Angels of Abundance

Grant Virtue

Copyright 2011 Grant Virtue. All rights reserved. No part of this book may be reproduced by any mechanical, photographic, or electronic process, or in the form of a phonographic recording; nor may it be stored in a retrieval system, transmitted, or otherwise be copied for public or private use – other than for

"fair use" as brief quotations embodied in articles and reviews – without written permission of the author.

The author of this book does not dispense medical advice or prescribe the use of any techniques as a form of treatment for physical, emotional, or medical problems without the advice of a physician, either directly or indirectly. The intent of the author is only to offer information of a general nature to help you in your quest for emotional and spiritual wellbeing. In the event that you use any of the information in this book for yourself, which is your constitutional right, the author assumes no responsibility for your actions.

ISBN 13: **978-1460949115**
ISBN 10: **1460949110**

To God, the source of all riches and abundance

Table of Contents

Introduction

Chapter One - What is Manifestation?

Chapter Two – Visualization

Chapter Three – Affirmations

Chapter Four - Prayer

Chapter Five - Keeping Your Focus

Chapter Six - Staying Positive

Chapter Seven - The Contract

Chapter Eight - Manifestation Stories

Chapter Nine - Meditations

Conclusion

Journal

About the Author

Introduction

Abundance is the natural state of being for us to be in. We are constantly surrounded by divine beings that want to protect and nurture us. These being go by many names and serve various roles. These beings are most commonly called by the name Angels.

The Angels of Abundance specifically refers to the cluster of angels that are specifically in charge of ensuring that our divine mission here on Earth is not hampered by lack. At different times abundance means very different things and this group of beings is responsible for ensuring that whatever need you have that you feel is being unfulfilled is taken care of.

Some of the angels that you can call upon for help whenever you need assistance with abundance are; Archangel Raphael, who ensures that your health in every aspect of your life is sound; Archangel Michael, who strives to protect you always and in all ways; Archangel Metatron, who has given us the gift of the platonic solids to expand our consciousness and reach untold heights of success; Archangel Raziel, the keeper of the mysteries, including alchemy, that can unlock the riches of the past; and Archangel Jophiel, who clears out all blockages preventing us from living an abundant and blessed life.

This is a book about contracts. The contracts in question are on the surface the same as any other contract you may be familiar with. They are between two or more interested parties who have something to offer one another. These contracts can be renegotiated at any time and each party hopes that the other will fulfill the terms.

However these contracts do have some dramatic differences from the sheaves of paper you have signed before. The first major difference you are likely to notice is that only one of the people behind this contract is, strictly speaking, a human. The renegotiation I mentioned earlier? That can only happen from one party, you. Perhaps the most striking difference of all is that you are making these contracts with every word, every thought, day by day.

In this book I will show you how, with surprisingly little effort on your part, you can make sure that these contracts go your way every single time. This is not a book about cutthroat tactics and getting ahead by standing on the backs of others. Quite the opposite in fact. This is as much a love story as it is a book about money.

You may be asking yourself, as Tina Turner did years ago, 'What's Love Got to Do With it?" Well, everything in fact. Throughout these next six chapters you will become quite familiar with how closely connected love and money truly are. I don't just mean in the sense that 'All is Fair in Love and Money' either, and rest assured that I certainly I do agree with The Beatles' early assertion that money cannot buy love.

Every single living person on this planet, or any other planet for that matter if it ever comes to that, is quite capable of mastering these techniques within a very short period of time. Nothing that I or anyone else can do in the realm of spirituality is beyond your grasp. All too often it seems that we grow quite dependent upon the guru to solve our problems, however since the guru did not create our problems the logic of that simply does not add up. It is up to us to use the skills we have been given by our creator to solve any problem that may crop up. I intend to help you remember how to use those skills.

Yes, remember. You see all of the information contained in this book is inherently known by each of us. We come to the planet knowing it, but gradually forget it. However not everyone forgets it at the same speed. The information can also be retained and relearned through meditation and disciplined praying. However nearly all of it can be learned by watching children, or by reading ancient texts in new ways. Some people would rather have that information presented simply and without dogma, and I do my best to provide.

One very important fact that I believe bears repeating is that all of us have within us the capability to be as wealthy as we desire. Not one of us needs to be downtrodden and beset with poverty for one day longer. All of us can earn as much money as we could ever need without having to sell our soul in the bargain. One does not need to act in a devious or unethical manner to obtain wealth. Truth be told acting in such a way is a sure fire way to ensure that whatever wealth you do obtain will be transient at best.

I would like to stress however that because this is a book about contracts you will be expected to hold up your end of the bargain for this to work. It is highly unlikely that you will have a dump truck full of $100 bills left in your driveway when you wake up in the morning, so you will at some point have to have some sort of gainful employment. Whether that is a traditional job, self-employment or a lemonade stand is not all that important. What is important is that you have some viable means of income that can stand to be larger and earn you more than it is now.

Throughout this book I will use terms such as the creator, the universe, the divine spirit and other such things. Feel free to translate these words into whatever makes you feel most comfortable. Regardless if you prefer the term God, Jesus, Buddha, Allah, Krishna or any other name everything contained in this book will work just the same. After all, they all mean the same thing - Love.

This book is for anyone who does not want their finances to limit how far they can go in life, a person that wants to help as many people as possible but simply lacks the funds for their vision. This book is also for those particular people that want to drive sports cars, race jet skis and obtain obscenely large houses. Those people also have much to offer the world; we just have to make sure they are not bored.

Finally this book is especially for those people who on first glance of this book upon the shelf thought to themselves "That book is too expensive!" No one reader will be helped more than this person, and if you ever do happen to meet that reader please buy them a copy as soon as possible. I can assure you that their gratitude will more than cover the cost.

I wish you good luck and good health on this journey you are about to undertake. The person reading this introduction will not be the same person reading the conclusion. You will not have been able to finish this book without undergoing that essential epiphany that will be required of you to truly manifest your desires. Don't believe me? Read on. Not sure what manifest means? Read on. Above all else, dear reader, please enjoy, for this instruction manual has only one goal in mind: To make your life better.

Chapter One

What is Manifestation?

"Let the beauty of what you love be what you do" - Jalal ad-Din Rumi

Regardless of which area you are in need of help, the angels are always waiting to assist you. There is no matter too great or too small for them to give you loving guidance and support. You simply need to ask them for this help.

Asking for help from the angels can come in many different forms. These forms are entirely dependent upon you, as the angels themselves do not particularly care to stand upon ritual or dogma.

In the case of this book we are primarily working with the Angels of Abundance. To ease you through the task in asking these particular angels for help we will use a basic set of terms that most people find comfortable and fitting. If you do not agree with these terms feel free to replace any word with one that makes you feel better. The first word that we will be using to ask the angels for help is called Manifestation.

Manifestation, at its very core and basic level, is essentially the result of a working agreement between yourself and the creator. Manifestation can reveal itself to be money, health, happiness, possessions or love. These things could not have come without you, and they in all likelihood would never appear without the creator. Manifestation is at its core what is negotiated in all divine contracts. It is the order you are placing with the universe, one which is delivered with all of the enthusiasm of a small child presenting a painting to a parent.

Manifestation however comes with one very major caveat; you get exactly what you order, every single time, without exception. There has never been a case in human history where a person was rich, poor, or somewhere in between where they did not at some point wish themselves into that state of being. I realize that this may seem exceptionally cold to some people, after all who would wish themselves poor? The answer is that we all do from time to time. Very few among us have never in a private moment of self-pity bemoaned our situation, or thought to ourselves unworthy of success.

While we are human and these thoughts will always be a part of our lives, we must take steps to minimize them. There is, of course, no thought police checking to make sure that you think happy thoughts. The creative genius of Rod Serling notwithstanding, no one will have to be banished to a cornfield for thinking incorrectly. No one will even know if you are getting down on yourself and thinking negatively. No one is trying to tell you how to speak, how to act or how to think.

If, however, you do desire to change your life for the better and remove the negative habits of your past forever you will need to start changing the way you think and the way you speak. While you are not going to get into trouble for speaking or thinking negatively, you will quickly start to realize that every time you do it is a wasted opportunity. No situation on Earth can be improved by worrying or complaining, whilst most any situation can certainly be improved by looking at it positively.

Why is this? Primarily improvement comes from the fact that if you look at a situation positively, you are acknowledging that it is has hope. That allows you to think creatively to work out a situation, instead of just declaring the whole thing hopeless and giving up. Let us not also diminish the practical consideration that positive people are a much greater joy to spend time with than people we perceive to be complainers or excessively negative. We are much more likely to go out of our way to help people who are positive and are taking active steps to improve their lives, and likewise other people are much more likely to help us when we are trying to look on the brighter side of life. Beyond the practical implications however are the spiritual considerations of our thoughts and words.

During the course of writing and researching for the book "Angel Words", it was discovered that the words we say and how we say them have a real energy to them. Positive words contain a far higher energy than negative words, and thus have a far greater impact on the world around us. Every word that we utter leaves our mouths at over seven hundred miles per hour. Crystal glass will actually be etched at the microscopic level by sounds, and it can only be assumed that all physical objects being so closely related on an atomic level react in a similar, if not identical, manner. Since it has long been proven through neuroscience that our thoughts likewise contain energy it would not be a far leap to suggest that positive thoughts are higher in energy than negative thoughts.

If we can, at least temporarily, accept all of this business about energy at face value then it says quite a lot about how we go about manifesting what we really desire and not what we would rather avoid. Fortunately for us because positive words and thoughts are so much more powerful than negative ones that we can instantly negate any potentially nasty thing coming our way by turning it around to being positive as soon as we recognize the negative thought or word.

Perhaps the easiest way to think of manifesting is if we look at it as if we would a meal. No, we do not intend to eat this particular thing although it is not outside the realm of possibility that we could indeed manifest ourselves a nice meal. No, for this exercise it is a meal in a metaphorical sense only. This particular restaurant we received this meal at has the most extensive menu you could possibly imagine. Nearly any food conceived of by man is present on this menu. It sounds great, but the twist is that the wait staff is completely without opinions of their own. You could order the most awful thing and they would not blink their eyes at it. Likewise you could order the specialty of the house and get no more reaction from the fellow taking your order. It is their desire to simply serve you that overrides any warning. If you ordered that Steak Tartar when you actually wanted Eggplant Parmesan, well then they just assume that what you said is what you meant. So it is with our lives.

Specificity must become job number one then when we are working to achieve a goal. We must not falter in our absolute conviction that it will succeed, that it can be salvaged and that it must work. While it is not the end of the world if we do stumble, we must remember that ultimately we are our only taskmasters in this world and we must strive to discipline ourselves to the point where stumbling into negative thinking is the exception and not the rule. Again, you will not be punished by anyone for faltering but when you consider the opportunity lost that in itself can be disciplining enough.

Nearly everyone should be by now familiar with the term "Be careful what you wish for." Nowhere is this truer than when you are trying to manifest your desires. The reason is that you never know when you are going to get that thing you are thinking about. It could be good, it could be bad but in any case you never know when or if it is going to show up. Now most of the time it is only the good things that come into our lives, however from time to time we do manage to put in that order for the foul tasting food and it comes back to us. However every single time you wish for something good to come into your life it will come to you.

Now this may seem surprising to you because surely at some point in your life you wished for something and it certainly did not come to you. Why was this? A number of factors could have affected that particular wish. Perhaps you did not want it as much as you really thought, so even though you did want it at one point in time you had really changed your mind by the time it was going to come your way. Maybe you simply lost hope or focus and as they say "gave up five minutes before the miracle." Most likely whatever it was that you wished for simply would not have served a higher purpose in your life. Essentially it was not good for you. Whatever may have happened, it is important to not think of that instance as the time you tried to manifest and failed. Even if the reason is not known to you and I why it did not work rest assured that there is a very good reason none the less.

Dwelling on the reasons you did not get what you want is not going to help you at any point in your life, let alone in manifesting true wealth. It is far more important to focus on the future in a bright and optimistic way. Keeping yourself in a positive state of mind helps ensure that you are only bringing into your life that which you truly want, not that which you fear. Fear must be overcome precisely because we as human beings are so wonderful at bringing about what we think of most. Fortunately for us all we are being looked after by divine beings every minute of every day, and as such do not have any real reason to be afraid. Keeping that in mind at all times should allow you to forget all of those things you would rather not have in your life and leave you room to only focus on that which serves you best. During those times when you are not feeling your best, or you feel a bit down about your situation, it is especially vital that you keep firm track of your thoughts and words. It is at times when we are under the sway of particularly strong emotions that our thoughts and words manifest the quickest. The reason why, is that it is at those times when we are most convinced of what we want and are therefore the clearest in our desires.

There are various tools and techniques you can use to increase the chances that your manifestation will happen more quickly and more accurately. These focusing devices come in all shapes and forms and the actual device is not quite as important as is the person's belief that is using it. One particular tool that has come back into popular use in the recent years for manifestation is the quartz crystal. Users believe that this particular crystal has an amplifying ability that somehow increases the power of your thoughts and desires. The actual process that takes place could most probably fill an entire book on its own but if the proof is in the doing you could certainly experiment with one of these crystals with very little effort or expense. The basics of the technique are to hold the crystal in your right hand, your so called giving hand, and focus on your desire. If you are having trouble keeping focus on what it is you want you may want to try something called 'visualization', a subject that will be explained quite thoroughly in the next chapter. Once you have found your focus you will want to keep that in your mind for as long as you desire while holding that crystal.

There are of course places where crystal grows naturally and simply being around them is enough of a focusing tool for most people. A good example of this is a particular rocky outcropping in the small California town of Laguna Beach which is locally known as the 'manifestation rocks.' The reason they have received this moniker is because of the fact that they are absolutely studded with small quartz crystals. I personally know of a great many people who make weekly treks out to this outcropping to focus on what they would like to bring into their lives. Regardless of the weather, such as it is in southern California anyhow, they will be out there with pens and journals to help them remember all those things they wished for.

Naturally a person does not require focusing tools to be able to manifest. It is something that happens anyway. However some people do find that they are able to visualize their goals much more clearly when they have something physical to hold and see. We will go into the subject of visualization in much greater detail later, however suffice it to say that those of us without highly trained imaginations find it much easier to think of an object when we can see a close approximation of it. That is more or less the entire point of my previous book, "Angel Blessings Candle Kit". In that book we used candles as focusing devices to help us manifest what we most desired.

If any of this sounds difficult so far please know that the actual practice is very simple indeed. Like anything of course practice does make it easier and more effective, but this is practice that you will come to enjoy very much. Why? Because the rewards are so many and so easily obtainable.

By now you should have a fairly firm grasp on what this manifesting business is all about, as well as a general impression on how to go about doing it. In the next few chapters we will go into much more detail on exactly how to go about manifesting with the least amount of effort and the maximum amount of results.

Chapter Two

Visualization

The Angels of Abundance want to make your life as easy as possible. They help us achieve our goals by assisting us in visualizing our desires. They know that what we visualize we will receive and so they gently remind us to always visualize positive, loving images that we truly do desire. It is primarily for this reason that the angels encourage us to stay away from images and movies that depict hurtfulness or violence. The angels want us to see things that bring us joy, rather than pain.

Visualization is one of those topics that has been covered by several spiritual and new age authors. In some notable cases the topic of visualization has taken the form of quite large books. Most of the time these books deal primarily with what is called "Positive Visualization." That is picturing what you want so you have a clearer picture of how to obtain it. For our purposes we are going to use visualization in a similar method as described in those books, however do not fear if you have never read any of this information before. Throughout this chapter you will become well versed in the art of visualization, with no prior experience needed.

Some of you may be unfamiliar with the whole subject of visualization, and that is perfectly fine. Fortunately for all of us it is a remarkably simple thing not only to explain but to practice. Throughout this book I will strive to make the practice as effortless as humanely possible. There will be times where that does not seem to be the case and there I will strive to show you what I mean by the word "effortless". While it is entirely possible to make visualization into something complicated and unapproachable, I can assure you that it is most likely something you are already doing. As I stated previously every one of us were born with this knowledge, some of us just forgot how to use it. Evidence the fact that children seem to have remarkable imaginations in comparison to adults. Is this because we gradually become enthralled to the "real world" or could it possibly be because we slowly start to forget that our world is not the only "real world" in existence? It is precisely the time when we forget or deny that magic does indeed exist that we force ourselves into living with only the day to day existence of our modern world. Truth be told I can certainly understand the arguments that many would put forward that they simply have not got the time for such childish nonsense. True that may be, the fact that they haven't got the time has much more to do with the fact that they are so enraptured with the "real world" that they cannot fathom another exists and refuse to use the tools available from that other world to make sure that they do indeed have the time.

Visualization is simply a method of calling up a picture in your mind. Yes, it is that simple. Picture what you had for breakfast this morning in as much detail as you can manage. Picture the dish you used, the utensils you ate with. Imagine the texture, the taste and smell of this food. Can you really see that meal in your mind? Is it so real you can almost grab it?

Congratulations, that is visualization! Don't fret if you did not manage to get very much detail into your mind with that last exercise, this technique does require practice to perfect. Yes the practices may take a little bit of work but consider this training for your new job. What new job might this be you ask? The job of manifesting your desires, not only at times when you find yourself wanting or needing something in particular, but every minute of every day. Once you perfect the techniques in this book you will realize the fact that you are nearly always visualizing, and nearly always manifesting. The truth of the matter is that you always have been as well.

Whenever I feel that I am not achieving the level of detail I desire I like to perform a special training technique. What I do is find an object that I am quite familiar with, and picture it in my head for a few minutes. I try to picture it with as much detail as I can remember and then compare that to the real object in front of me. If I missed something important I study that bit and try again, seeing if I can really get a dramatically detailed image. Yes this may sound astonishingly simplistic but I do find that the beginning is often the best place to start.

If for any reason you were not happy with the level of detail or even your ability to conjure up in your mind the picture you were trying to achieve, the time to work on this is now. This is one area where you will almost certainly want to make sure that you have down pat before you proceed. I do understand that while the above practice may be easy it can also be time consuming. It can be a challenge to fit yet another thing in to your already busy schedule. However there are a couple things to consider when planning time to practice. The first is that you can practice this technique most anywhere. Sure, visualizing while driving may be quite dangerous but you can definitely try it during your lunch hour. You can even practice while you are lying in bed at night; it can even be quite relaxing and conducive to sleep. The second thing to take into consideration is that the payoff for learning this technique can be quite extraordinary.

The reason I encourage you to practice your visualization so often is simple: If you are happy with the amount of detail that you are achieving then it makes it all that much easier for you. You do not want to be distracted with wishing that you were a better visualizer. The quality of the visual that you were able to conjure up really does have a lot to do with how well you manifest at times. Certainly for highly detailed, and specific, things that you are trying to manifest you will want that much detail. After all if you are very clear on the fact that you want a 2008 Chevrolet Corvette as opposed to a 2007, you will have to be a lot more specific with your picture than most people. Likewise if you are manifesting a job it is highly recommended that you try to achieve as specific a picture in your mind as possible. Employment and housing are two areas in particular where "almost" is simply not good enough.

In my experience there is one area in particular that most people seem to worry about, that is somehow doing something wrong. To be perfectly honest the only thing wrong a person can do in regards to manifesting is to not try. It is when we forget that we have this power that people tend to slip into negativity and accidentally manifest for themselves all sorts of things that they never would actually want. Take the case of what society would dub a "worrywart." For those of you who may be unfamiliar with this term it is typically defined as a person who worries excessively or without cause. I am sure that at some point in your past or present you have known or currently know someone who would fit this description accurately. The quite unfortunate thing for them is that while they may have the very best intentions, the constant worrying and fretting can inadvertently attract some of the very same things that they seem to be living their life in terror of in the first place. However had they been aware of this fact you would most likely find that most people would avoid this type of excessive worrying almost without fail.

Some people find the use of physical pictures to be immensely helpful. If you are a particularly visual person you may find it useful to obtain a cork board from your local office supply store and tack up pictures of those things you are trying to manifest. This achieves two goals; first it helps you remember what they look like with a great deal of accuracy, and second it reminds you to always focus on those things that you desire most. Having a scattered focus can be useful at times, but when it comes to visualizing and manifestation sometimes the best thing you can do is to hone in on something like a laser beam.

While you are visualizing what you desire or need you are in the process of manifestation. It really can be that simple and effortless. The more you focus on it the more you can fine tune exactly what will come to you in your life. Certainly free will and plain old randomness will bring you to certain situations that you most certainly did not manifest, but when we are talking about that tricky subject called

"luck" we are really speaking of manifestation. Does this mean you will win the lottery if you manifest it? Maybe, but most likely not. What is at play with the lottery and gambling in general is a form of mechanics that cannot be easily manipulated using spiritual powers. Rather what we are discussing here is the type of thing people typically chalk up to luck when they receive a random refund from their utility company in the mail.

Believe it or not this is exactly the type of thing that typically happens to people when they start to manifest abundance. Some people get anonymous checks in the mail, or perhaps their payment to their utility company comes back but the credit is applied all the same. Perhaps they get hired for a small side job at precisely the time when they need a bit of extra money. This is not to say, of course, that a person could not manifest substantially more money than these token payments. Since this abundance is nothing more than a gift from the universe the actual amount is not limited in any real way.

So how does one go about achieving these sorts of massive boosts through visualization? Simple, dream big! If you want to be the CEO of a company you don't apply for the mail room, you apply for the big job. Sure you may not get it when the mail room would be a sure thing but the chance is worth the risk. The same basic principle applies here as well. If you want to manifest a bestselling book then the best place to start is to visualize yourself as a bestselling author. You will need to really see yourself writing the book, deciding on the subject, setting the chapters and everything that goes along with the writing process. You will also need to be particularly vigilant as to how you visualize yourself after the book is finished. Can you really see yourself on television, writing articles and giving talks about your book? Fantastic! If not, you will need to practice seeing this in as detailed a fashion imaginable. This is the same pattern of visualization that you will use regardless of whatever big dream you would like to have come true. You really have to believe it is not only true, but the only possible outcome. The reason you need to do all of these things is that you are putting an order in with the universal chef, and you don't want that order to come back to you wrong or incomplete. The bigger we dream the more specificity is required of us.

The more that you visualize the easier it becomes. This may sound trivial at first glance, and especially before you try of the techniques outlined above. It sounds almost too easy to sit and think of yourself in wonderful situations where there are no problems. You would be correct in that assumption as well, it is incredibly easy and effortless to do so. However it is easier for some people than others, but everyone can get to the same level of expertise. The actual practice of visualizing is so easy that everyone already does it every single day. However what can take practice is again bringing the visualizations up to the level of detail required so that you do get exactly what you would like. You are free of course to get by with 'good enough' in your visualizations, and to a point that is what everyone does. Since there will always be room for improvement at some point you will have to say that you are content with the level of detail obtained and try in earnest to visualize and manifest something without it just being "practice."

When visualizing it is important to remember that just because something can go wrong, it never needs to go wrong. Certainly having a backup plan is never a bad thing in this world but your visualizations are always going to be best case scenarios. Of course there are other people in this world with their own goals and ambitions, and some of those people may not be as caring and nice as you are when it comes to competition but those people really are their own problems and you do not have to constantly think up contingencies. If their machinations come into conflict with the end result of your manifestations, just trust that they have their own karma and just release all negative thoughts and emotions about them to the universe. This business of manifestation is all about positivity, where you simply do not have time to think or dwell on negative people and situations.

The give you a brief idea of exactly how powerful a tool visualization is, we will temporarily depart from the area of manifesting abundance and into the realm of health. Since these are incredibly connected areas of our lives I ask your forgiveness this brief digression. My wife's close friend years back was diagnosed with cancer. This can be a traumatic experience in itself, but as this lady was also a professional dancer losing her physical health also meant losing her sole source of income as well. As great as dance companies may be, they are not known for providing their members with health insurance. This was a good and talented person who honest to goodness could not afford to be sick.

Over the course of weeks and months she gradually got worse and worse until the point where the doctors had essentially let her know to make sure that all of her affairs were in order. Rather than give into despair she decided to change the course of her life and refuse to accept and give into illness. She proceeded to see herself as completely healed. She could feel herself dancing, hear the crowd cheering, and could visualize herself growing old. Her faith in this healing was so strong that she would never believe that any other alternative was possible.

As you can probably guess she was completely healed of this formerly terminal cancer a very short while later. It has not returned, and nor is it likely to. Just because the doctors had given up on her did not mean that she had to as well. The power of this healing is immense, not only in its scope but also its implications. The most remarkable thing about it was how utterly effortless the healing was. Through sheer faith and not a small bit of stubbornness she was able to become a free person once again. How much smaller is the simple act of creating abundance in our lives? If visualization and manifestation can do something so incredibly powerful why would anyone ever think that they would not be able to simply get a better job, a raise or start a business of their own?

The power of visualization is limited only by the belief of the person who is using the tool. If you can see something happen, it can happen. You can therefore see why with an increased power of imagination your potential for manifestation increases as well. It is for this reason that any exercise to increase your imagination should be pursued with all of the seriousness of any university course. Simple and pleasurable tasks such as reading fantasy and science fiction, or playing board and computer role playing games can be incredibly beneficial in encouraging imagination. Of course as with all other things it is important to use these tools in moderation. It would not benefit anyone to spend every waking moment trapped inside a fantasy story. However if done properly these books and games can help you develop a boundless sense of scope and wonder. This is precisely where you should be.

You may at some point wonder if it is possible to use the power of visualization for some negative purpose. After all there are unfortunately people who do not have the highest good of humanity in mind and would attempt to press any potential advantage, spiritual or physical. Fortunately for the rest of us the answer is a very firm 'No.' As I explained in my previous books, "Angel Blessings Candle Kit" and "Angel Words" negative thoughts, words and energies carry far less energy than positive ones. This means that while it is theoretically possible for someone to manifest something negative, chances are incredibly likely that the power of the rest of us visualizing positive changes for the world would completely overpower the negative. In "Angel Words" it was demonstrated precisely how comparatively weak negativity is. It is vitally important to learn exactly how little power negativity has, so that you are not afraid of it. When we give fear to negativity we increase its power and ironically turn it into something that we ought to fear. When we realize how little power negativity has in the first place we can ignore it or scoff at it, limiting its power that much further. One simple prayer for peace, healing, and abundance for all a day is more than enough to counter whatever negative plots anyone may be hatching.

As contrary as it may sound it is indeed possible to spend too much time visualizing goals and not enough time attaining them. As I stated in the introduction of this book, this whole business of manifesting abundance is a contract. This does mean that you will have to hold up your end of the bargain. We certainly can make manifesting this abundance effortless, by transforming the things that you were doing anyway into being much more effective. However you will need to allow yourself to accept the incoming abundance by creating an avenue for it to come to you. This means you will either need to have a job, your own business or some creative project that you intend to sell for monetary gain. While it is very nice to have a private poetry journal, or doodle on the back of napkins it is unlikely that either of those will make you rich unless you first set out to ensure that they are seen and read by the world. If for any reason you have any qualms about work, business ownership or having the world see and judge your creative projects you will need to move through those blockages before you will be able to continue.

In the next chapter I will illustrate exactly how to ensure that you are ready to receive all of the abundance that is coming your way.

Chapter Three

Affirmations

The Angels of Abundance love the use of affirmations. They feel that any sort of positivity in our lives is such a beautiful thing, that saying positive words repeatedly is that much more beautiful. The Angels of Abundance encourage us to speak only loving and healing words at all times, but especially in our affirmations.

Like all angels, the Angels of Abundance are messengers. They hear our affirmations and relay them back to our creator for the desires to be granted. When we give them positive affirmations to deliver they do so with much more enthusiasm and speed than they would if we only gave them negative affirmations. Throughout this chapter keep in mind the sort of messages that you would like to deliver, and try to avoid anything that would make you as a messenger cringe.

Affirmations can best be described as sayings that you tell yourself until you believe them. These sayings are not outright false, however. They are quite true, however sometimes they are just not true yet. The value in these sayings is that they prepare your mind for success when sometimes through societal, familial and personal influences we are not ready to accept it. Another positive benefit of the affirmation is that, like visualization, you are defining exactly what you would you like to attain. Whether this is a beautiful house, a bestselling novel, a giant raise or even increased skill at automotive repair anything you would like to obtain can in part be achieved by saying out loud to yourself and the universe.

A typical affirmation goes something like this, "I have a bestselling book. I am a bestselling author." It can be as simple as that and usually the simpler the better. The basic formula of the affirmation requires that you use the present tense for the most part. The reason for this is that your status as a bestselling author must be established now, not some nebulous point in the future. If you are trying to achieve something on a specific date it would be permissible to say for example, "I will get a large raise in one months' time." This would take into account your companies typical schedule of adjusting pay rates, and would be much more convincing to yourself that using the present tense.

In my first example above I used the affirmation, "I have a bestselling book. I am a bestselling author." The wording here is more precise than would appear at first glance. It could certainly look like a redundancy to someone looking at it from a purely logical frame of mind. However upon closer examinations you will note that this is actually two affirmations in one. The first is that the book you are attempting to sell is a bestseller. That is great news and something to be proud of. The second is that you are a bestselling author. This would imply that all of your books you intend to sell will be bestsellers. You can see why this double affirmation would be that much more powerful than simply stating, "I have a bestselling book." We are going for massive abundance here. On the same token you could say, "I have sold my first painting. I am a popular, professional artist." would achieve much the same effect for those in the art field. For someone who is gainfully employed a similarly effective affirmation would go something like, "I will get a large raise in one months' time. I am a valued and critical employee." Of course this method is not required, and there is absolutely nothing wrong with stating only one affirmation at a time, I simply have found the double affirmation technique to be far more effective in the long run. You are encouraged to try both methods and use the one that feels the best to you.

You will want to repeat this to yourself a number of times throughout the day. If for one reason or another you are unable to repeat this mantra to yourself through the course of the day, it is still beneficial to repeat it at at least one point. Some people I know use the time at night when they are getting ready to go to bed to start saying their affirmations. In many circles the nightly affirmation has replaced the prayer before bed that was typical Americana until recent times. The repetition is important because as marketing folks are so often telling us, it takes several tries before our brain really absorbs a message. However once it is absorbed it tends to stay absorbed.

One may start to wonder how long exactly they will be expected to repeat these affirmations. Fortunately they do come with an expiration date. In the example of "I have a bestselling book. I am a bestselling author." it would bear repeating until the fact was firmly established as truth. When your first and second bestsellers are on the market you can pretty much assume that your affirmation has taken. Of course you are not under any sort of obligation to stop the affirmation at that point, and indeed the idea of quitting a winning strategy has dubious merits at best, but you can at least be assured that you can stop and still have achieved your goal. If you were using the affirmation, "I will get a large raise in one months' time" and at the end of that month you do indeed get your large raise, why not keep it up? If your company does not do monthly pay rate adjustments it would be a trivial modification of your established affirmation to take into account the next pay adjustment period. Obviously since this technique is largely designed to benefit you in your life, you are free to choose to start and stop at any time without fear of reproach or judgment by any other person.

Affirmations are not limited to simple abundance sayings. Anything at all you would like to do in this world can be made easier, better and faster by using affirmations. You could even, for example, have an affirmation that in ceases the yield of your vegetable garden. Saying "My vegetable garden is highly productive. I am a wise and knowledgeable gardener." can and will produce some fantastic results. Along those lines, anything you can think of can be made into an affirmation.

You might have already guessed then how affirmations and visualization work together. As was stated in the previous chapter your success with visualization is entirely dependent on your imagination, and through visualization you can increase the power of your imagination. You may also be able to say that your affirmations are dependent on your visualizations. Before you can come up with an affirmation you must know what it is that you are trying to achieve. The best way to find out what you are trying to achieve is to visualize it in detail. It is possible and indeed highly likely that by using your affirmations regularly you will even be able to visualize your goal with heightened clarity. This is achieved because by using constant affirmations we are getting our brain used to the idea of our goal. The more familiar we are with this goal the better able we are to visualize it as completed. The more you affirm the better your visualizations will be and the more you visualize the more effective your affirmations will be.

Affirmations are considered effortless because they can be done anywhere. While performing them in public you may be accused of talking to yourself or some such thing, but anywhere where you can talk you can manifest. Our brains are also remarkable in that they can multitask in amazing ways. There are very few activities that saying affirmations would interfere with. Likewise there are very few jobs that a person would find it inappropriate to perform affirmations during. Often you will find that jobs encourage affirmations and even have a few that the higher ups themselves often use. This is particularly true in sales fields and sports teams. While this may seem esoteric to some of the uninitiated at your office, in our capitalist society we value results far above mere skepticism and propriety. If your public affirmations result in even 1% higher sales figures for you I can guarantee your coworkers and employers will quickly change their attitude and belief towards these remarkable tools.

Obviously a 1% increase in anything isn't all that much, but it does help to illustrate how small a margin it takes for someone to go from a disbeliever to a practitioner. Imagine then how much more seriously your coworkers will take you when you start achieving closer to 25% or more increase in your income? Of course this is just an example, as not everyone is in sales, however if you can figure out a way to measure your success in the work place it can be increased through affirmations.

While you are reading this chapter I would like for you to try this simple affirmation, "I am capable and deserving of achieving all of this and more." Periodically repeat this to yourself and see how quickly you attain a result. You will know you have had a result because some form of unexpected abundance will come your way. Obviously this can take drastically different forms depending on the individual person but you should be able to recognize it when it comes. As for how much time it is likely to take that is up to the universe, but generally speaking when we start with affirmations the results can be incredibly fast.

In some ways however affirmations work in a similar way to advertising, that is you do the affirmation now and the results happen later. This can lead to a "lag time" in which it could be interpreted that nothing is happening. Once you are over the hurdle there will be a nearly constant visual effect of your past efforts. If you were to stop at this point you would still see an effect for a time until the abundance catches up with the affirmations that you already tried. This is an easy mistake to make because it can appear that we can suddenly become complacent and still reap the benefits.

It is for this reason that I would really encourage you to keep the "lag time" in mind.

When discussing these techniques with skeptics and the uninitiated it does help to remind them that the act of affirmation does not contradict any religious practice. It is an entirely non-denominational act that will not cause them to have to renounce or affirm any believe in any organization or belief structure. They certainly will not be punished for trying these techniques. On the contrary they will be able to reap rewards for their efforts. The theological considerations behind the reason for the rewards can often vary dramatically between different people and different belief structures. For the most part I recommend avoiding that area of it as it is most decidedly subjective in nature. You can of course enter into any sort of debate as you wish, but it is far better to go into any discussion of that sort armed with the knowledge that no one person will ever know all there is to know about divine intervention. How it works and why it works are most decidedly topics for the grand theological societies and universities to tackle, it is sufficient enough for our purposes that it does work.

Affirmations can be generally placed in one of three different categories. Those categories being:

1. Constant Affirmations
2. Acquisition Affirmations
3. Emergency Affirmation

Obviously from time to time you will be able to find affirmations that can be made that do not fit into any of the categories, but for the purposes of this chapter we will primarily focus on these three.

The first category is called Constant Affirmations because these are the type of affirmations that a person does on a regular basis. "I am an effective manager", "I have an excellent sales record" are both examples of the constant affirmation category. This category is particularly useful for maintaining or gradually increasing the level of productivity or abundance in your life. By regularly repeating such positive phrases you are training your brain and the universe that this really is what you want and the minimum you are willing to accept. The reason these phrases would not fit into the other two categories is that it does not dress a specific or urgent need. Affirmations that fall under the "Constant Affirmation" heading are generally done for much of a person's life, or at least throughout their working career.

You can use the Constant Affirmation to maintain or benefit other areas of your life as well. It would be a perfectly acceptable and effective affirmation to state "I am a great father" or "My family life is peaceful, harmonious and fulfilling for us all." If you have any areas of your life that you have found to be a consistent challenge you can use this category of affirmations to fix those as well. The next time you are stressed about your commute try saying something along the lines of "My way to work is perfectly clear, safe and stress free."

For some people they may find the Constant Affirmation class a bit tedious or unfulfilling. Since this is not the type of affirmation one would preferably use to enact sweeping and radical changes in their life in a very short period of time it is particularly important to be patient here. Often times this category can show dramatic results but over a much longer timeline than some people would prefer. Also keep in mind that it is called "Constant" for a very good reason, in that these are sayings that you will want to repeat for the foreseeable future. There is no built in expiration date for these because who can really quantify what an effective manager or great dad really is? These are certainly understandable complaints but the long term benefits of this classification of affirmation cannot be denied. It is in everybody's best interest to start a constant affirmation and stick to it throughout their life. It is undeniably a task that requires discipline, and that can only lead to further financial gain.

There are times when a constant affirmation is not the right choice. For times when you need something done, and done now you would be much better served with other methods. Certainly you are free to try but the results may not be as dramatic or immediate as you desire. It would certainly be nice if one type of affirmation could apply in every single instance but that sadly is just not the case. With practice you will instinctually know when to use the constant affirmation and when to switch off to something more immediate.

The second classification of affirmation is called the "Acquisition Affirmation." These affirmations are used, as the name implies, to acquire specific things in your life. Any object that you desire will become yours with thoughtful application of this affirmation. You may be thinking to yourself, "Did I read that right? Surely he can't mean anything."

The answer is "Yes," you did read that right and you can absolutely acquire any physical object that you desire. Certainly there are limitations when it comes to people, sometimes a person desires another person but regardless of what they do the other person will not reciprocate. That cannot be fixed with this method, or any other that any sane person would bother with. However any tangible, non-sentient, object is within your grasp.

This principle works loosely based on the fact that every object, including you, is made up of microscopic atoms. All atoms at their very core are essentially magnetically charged. What this affirmation does is allow you to change the charge within yourself to become the polar opposite from that object, and thereby attract it. I realize that this sounds needlessly esoteric and you are free to ignore the reasons why this principle works or even supply an answer that satisfies you more. The fact that it does work is undeniable.

A simple acquisition affirmation would go something like this, "I have a brand new electric car." Or, "I have one-million dollars in my bank account." Again it is important to speak in the present tense with these affirmations. You are stating that you are in possession of this item now, not some indeterminate future. It helps to be very clear on what it is that you want. If you say, "I have a bunch of money" or "I have a car," what do those really mean? A bunch of money to you may be a trifling sum to others and vice versa, likewise a car can be anything from a Bentley to a beat up old Buick. In the realm of Abundance, Specificity is king.

These types of affirmations do not have any sort of built in timeline, unfortunately. You can try to put in an artificial timeline along the vein of "I will have a brand new car within two weeks." However that manipulation of the construct does violate one of the principle laws of affirmation, to speak in the present tense. Certainly you are free to try this little trick out and no harm will come to you as a result of this, but you may be disappointed by the results if you are holding too many expectations on the timeline. Patience is an incredibly valuable trait to possess when it comes to manifesting in all of its guises.

When we let go, and simply allow nature to take its course is when the most powerful magic happens. Forcing things into place is not a natural process and will ultimately lead to nothing. We must cultivate in ourselves a more natural timeline and let things come to us as they are needed, but be open to them when they do come.

Acquisition Affirmations are particularly powerful when seeking a new job or position. While the constant affirmation is terrific for maintaining and gradually improving a career, the acquisition affirmation is the go-to guy for dramatic upward progression. If you feel that you have languished for too long in one position that is far below your skill set then the acquisition affirmation will allow you to have upward mobility without any risk of seeming too ambitious or ungrateful for what you currently have. Using this technique will allow you to entertain job offers from competitors or have a promotion spontaneously bestowed upon you.

If you are competing for a position that you feel you truly deserve more than anyone else does and you know when the decision is going to be made, the acquisition affirmation is not the best choice. Again, this affirmation class has no time limit or expiry date. What you are manifesting will come to you but the date is not certain. You can be assured that the time that it comes to you will be the best time imaginable for both yourself, the universe and the object in question but no one can ever tell you the exact time that is likely to happen.

The third classification of affirmation is called the "Emergency Affirmation." The term emergency here is used because of the necessary for timeliness, not to imply that someone is in any sort of danger. However if someone were faced with danger of any sort this would certainly be the affirmation to use. If, as in the previous example, you were attempting to gain recognition for a promotion that is definitely happening on a certain schedule this would be the affirmation to use. Affirmations of this type are unique in that they most certainly do have a time limit and expiration date.

A simple emergency affirmation would look something like this, "I am safe and surrounded by love now," or "I will be promoted at my job review next Tuesday." Like the previous classes of affirmation it is important to either use the present tense or specify an exact date. Using words such as "someday" or "soon" is a good way to go nowhere fast because no one knows when "someday" and "soon" really are. Do you remember when you were a kid and asked if you could do something and received a "Maybe," or "Soon" in response? It was probably pretty frustrating and may have left you a bit confused and unfulfilled. That is an instinctual response to the ambiguity of the words used. You naturally knew that the adults around you needed to be more specific to guarantee a desired result, however you probably had no idea why.

You might think that this is the type of affirmation to use in all scenarios; after all, we generally want things to happen straight away, right? That is a generally correct, but these types of emergency affirmations do not always work. The previous affirmation categories work every single time, without fail. The way they work is that they realign your body and mind to be attuned with the object of your desires. With

60

emergency affirmations there simply is not enough time for this process to complete. The emergency affirmation works more or less along the lines of a prayer. That is, you are asking that if it is in your higher good to have this thing that it comes to you now. You are letting God, the universe, whomever, that you are in need of divine intervention at this particular moment. Obviously sometimes the answer is going to be "No."

The intricacies of our lives are far too complex for us to see the entire picture. We rely on the divine to see what it is we need and then provide it. Sometimes though a bit of a push from us can jump start the process. We, as humans, are blessed with free will. The universe can generally intervene on our behalf when we ask. Of course if it is part of the divine contract we signed before we came down to Earth in the first place then it will happen anyway, a kind of fate if you will. When we use the emergency affirmation we are signaling that we are open to this help and need it now. This frees the universe to act on our behalf without risk of interfering with our free will, a rule that is never broken.

A combination of these three methods of affirmation with a healthy dose of accurate visualization can lead to untold wealth for you, not just physically but spiritually as well. Studies have shown that people who use affirmations regularly feel much more connected and at peace with their deities. The reason is that you really take a hand as a co-creator in your universe and life. The seeming randomness of the universe is more closely understood to be the sacred and intricate dance that it really is. Try some affirmations out and see what abundance you are able to create in your life.

Chapter Four

Prayer

All prayer brings joy to the Angels. As devoted and loving messengers of God the angels rejoice in any attempt on our part to come closer to our creator. If you are in any way uncomfortable with prayer because of past experiences or associations, the angels strongly encourage you to restart this conversation with God now. Doing so on your own terms will achieve dynamic results as well as go a long way towards healing any residual pain you may be carrying. The power of prayer is limitless.

It is important to note that we do not pray directly to the angels, even the Angels of Abundance. That would make no sense. They are to God as our arms or mouth are to us, important pieces but not the whole.

If you are confused by the subject of this chapter you are not alone. For so many people prayer is considered something for "emergency use only." Using prayer for something so mundane as asking for more money, a better job or a promotion may seem petty to some or blasphemous to others. Fortunately for us all this is simply not true.

Prayer is one of the most powerful methods of obtaining anything in this life. We were put here by a divine being along with everyone and everything else in existence. It stands to reason, then, that everything is within the reach of this creator and can be bestowed upon us if we have the foresight to ask and it is in our best interest to obtain those items.

We do have free will, for better or for worse. This means that while of course the divine knows exactly what is best for us it is not always free to intercede on our behalf. If for some reason the divine decided to roll out the red carpet of abundance and luxury for us, what lessons would we learn and could we possibly grow?

This does not mean that we must live a life of want and sufferance in order to learn, but we absolutely must learn to ask for the good things in our lives. Asking can be done in various manners. In some ways hard work is a way of asking, as you are showing that you are willing to work for what it is that you want. Each of us needs to take that first step in meeting the divine half way and we must decide for ourselves which way is most comfortable and natural for us.

When we pray we enter into a conversation with our divine source and we are given the opportunity to allow a power higher than us to provide for our well-being. Just as a good parent does not interfere in their children's social lives unless it is dangerous or they are asked, we must also ask for any help we want.

The method of prayer your use is completely up to you. You can pray to any divine being of love and light that you resonate with. It can be a silent prayer, a simple prayer, a verbose and noisy prayer or a solemn candlelight hymn. You are free to choose whether or not to pray in the confines of a temple or church, your home or the great outdoors. No matter how you choose to pray the outcome will be exactly the same. Some organized religions have very specific precepts on how to pray and if you choose to follow those, that is perfectly acceptable. Likewise if you choose to buck convention and pray how you feel you want to, that is just fine.

When praying for abundance it is less important to visualize what it is that you want than you may think. The reason for this is that the divine knows exactly what it is that you want. Your mind is generally a very secure barrier but when it comes to prayer, it may as well be an open book. For your own sake you may want to continue visualizing the object you would like because it does help keep your mind focused (more on this in the next chapter) but do not be too hard on yourself if you are not able to manage this every time.

It is possible to use prayer in lieu of any other method quite successfully. Since prayer is going straight to the divine source it generally is the most powerful of all methods. However because you are asking for assistance sometimes the answer will still be a no. With visualization and affirmation there is never a question of whether or not it is going to work, only how quickly. It is for these reasons that while it is perfectly fine for someone to only use prayer, it is generally recommended that they utilize a combination of everything.

If you find that prayer is so effective for you that you do not want to bother with the other methods at all, that is okay too. You are the only one keeping score as it were so no one will ever fault you for not using all of your tools if you prefer using one over another.

I have often heard from people that they are afraid of "bothering" whatever deity they are praying to with their requests. This is never the case. Your creator is anxiously waiting to help you in your life and any sort of communication from you is welcome at any time. The amount of love flowing forth from our divine parent is nearly overwhelming and the more you pray the more you will start to feel loved. You will soon grow to feel very comforted and supported and asking for help will become a natural thing to do.

Some people feel that they need to offer something in return for this divine help. Rest assured that this is in no way necessary for this purpose. It is wonderful to do kind acts and will make you feel great inside, but negotiation is not a part of prayer. I do not want to in any way convince you not to do any charitable acts if that is something you feel guided to do, of course, but do not let any perceived inability to perform any of those acts stop you from utilizing the power of prayer.

Prayer is the one method that I use more than any other. It is not because I find it more effective than the other methods but because it is what I am most comfortable with. I have very close friends that are not quite so comfortable with prayer however and they choose to use the other methods with great success. Once we feel at peace with the method that we are using we will start to have more success with it in general.

A typical abundance prayer of mine usually goes something like this, "G-d, I desire to have the time to teach and write. I feel the need to have more money available to me so that I can focus more of my time on these projects rather than working for someone else. Please help me earn more money so that I can reach more people. Thank you."

That was a rather simple example, but one that is good enough to work most of the time. It is sincere most importantly. You can make the prayer simpler, such as:

"Please help me obtain more money."

Or you can get very complicated with it. As mentioned above the most important part is that you are sincere in your prayer. When you really believe and are genuinely having an outpouring of faith miracles can and do happen. If, however, you are merely "testing the waters" to see if this prayer thing actually works then your results may not be quite so rewarding.

If at any time you feel uncomfortable with the idea of utilizing prayer to manifest abundance then it is imperative that you stop. The only reason to use this method is because it rings true to you and you feel at peace. If that is not the case then you should absolutely not use this method and instead switch to others. Out of the three main methods of manifestation this is the one that generally causes more consternation amongst beginners, as quite considerable resources have been utilized to regulate the use of prayer within the confines of organized religion. While those practices and organizations absolutely have their place, the cost has come at a bit of personal choice in some case.

When used properly the power of prayer can be used for much more than simple financial abundance, and in fact this would be considered one of its more minor tasks. This is fortunate for the purposes of us as manifesting abundance is the primary focus of this book and presumably the reader from time to time. However when you have learned the practice of prayer and have achieved a degree of success with it you may also noticed that every area of your life begins to improve.

The first non-financial area where people start seeing an improvement is their health. Let's face it your health is your wealth so this is no small matter. In some ways this health improvement is the primary benefit of prayer and it has been successfully utilized along these lines for untold centuries. Recently there has been a rash of studies about the efficacy of prayer in the medical field. The majority have "proven" that prayer does in fact have an effect, even when the subject in question does not know they are being prayed for and the people doing the praying do not know who they are praying for. This is pretty exciting stuff.

The studies have also come up with some other interesting data, particularly in the cases when prayer was not effective. This may sound odd to be interested in the failure rate of a practice but in this case it has led to some positive developments. The primary cause of failure, or so the studies have concluded, is that the prayer was done without belief. An insincere prayer is generally as effective as no prayer at all. Now some studies have been able to show that symptoms were worse when the prayer was insincere but this data is most likely skewed. It is highly unlikely that an energy force that responds well to loving prayer would punish an ill person because of the actions of another.

It is for this reason primarily that if you are going to pray that you at the very least keep an open mind about it. Sincerity does not mean that you have to join a religion or start praying regularly, it does not mean that you have to tell anyone what you are doing and it certainly does not mean that you have to change your life if you are not guided to. All sincerity means is that you believe that you are honestly engaging in conversation with a higher power and you believe that they have the power to help you.

Chapter Five

Keeping Your Focus

You may be thinking to yourself, "Hasn't he gone over this already?" and the truth is that yes, in the preceding chapters I have spoken about keeping your focus during visualization and affirmations. However this is such an important topic that it warrants a chapter of its very own.

Focus is the key to all manifestation and hence the key to all abundance. Much as I advise you to be as specific as possible when you manifest and say your abundance, focus is what ensures that you will receive exactly what you want. Keeping focus can be tricky at times, especially if you are new to this whole manifestation "thing." There have been several books written on the topic of increasing attention span and the various ailments that people have been diagnosed with that seem to prevent any sort of long term focus. The fact of the matter is that anyone, regardless of physical or emotional state can focus long enough to perform simple visualizations and affirmations. The key is to use certain tools and techniques to help you along the way.

The first tool that is absolutely essential for most people is a simple pen and pad of paper. Keeping extensive notes will not only help you remember what it is that you want to focus on, but can be an important tool to help you keep track of your progress. Every affirmation you want to perform, everything you want to visualize should go into that pad of paper. How you organize this book is completely up to you. I have taken the liberty of giving you ten blank pages at the back of this book for use as a notebook. This way you can keep your lessons and notes in the same place. Obviously you will run out of space quite quickly but it should give you enough time to find your own writing pad in the meantime.

I cannot emphasize enough how much keeping notes will help you out in your days and weeks ahead. It can be incredibly easy to put off this simple chore, but detailing what worked and what did not will help you hone your focus to a razor edge. The very act of keeping notes in the very first place will go a long way towards improving your focus by its self. When we sit down to write down our thoughts and activities we are exercising not only our memories, but the parts of our brain that allow us to focus on one single task. If you naturally have a hard time focusing then this simple exercise may take a bit longer for you. That is perfectly fine; no one is going to keep track of your speed.

If you are the type of person who likes to have multiple affirmations a week that you use on a rotating basis, writing down the affirmations and the corresponding days that you would like to use them is a good idea. In this way you will be able to keep a focus on the affirmation itself rather than having to figure out which one you are using today. Likewise with visualization, if you paste or draw a picture of what it is that you would like, or a close representation in cases of job advancement and less tangible goods, it will help you get right into the visualization rather than trying to remember exactly what the object of your desire looks like.

Other simple objects can help you retain your focus as well. In previous work, Angel Blessings Candle Kit, I illustrated how using a candle can help you keep your mind focused on your goals. The book went on to show the connection between colors and manifestation, which is also a very useful tool. For the purposes of this section we will use the candle simply as a focusing device. The advantage that a candle has is that it is a physical object that you can hold in your hand. You know it is there because you can see it and feel it. This will lend credibility to your affirmations in your subconscious. Also you can use specific candles for each object or goal you are trying to manifest, so that you ensure that your complete focus is on that one goal and in doing so it will prevent your mind from drifting.

The basic method for using a candle as a focusing device is laid out in these easy to remember steps below:

1. Choose a small candle that has never been used before. If you know the color you would like to use for your specific purpose use that, otherwise choose a white candle.
2. Clean the candle in a small bowl of salt water (you can make your own or use sea water if available). Dry thoroughly.
3. Hold candle and imagine the goal that you would like to achieve. If it is a specific item try to picture that item completely contained inside the candle, waiting to burst out.
4. Light the candle and allow it to burn down completely. Feel free to recite an affirmation at this point, or simply meditate on the object of your desires. This works especially well at bath times.

That really is all there is to using candles for manifestation. There are a few advanced techniques involving dressing the candle in oil, watching the way the flames flicker and of course using specific colors and wax but that is beyond the scope of this book. Please reference the Angel Blessings Candle Kit for more information.

Other devices that you can use to help keep focused are crystals. Crystals share common traits with candles, in that since they are physical items that you can hold you are more able to focus on the real practical applications of what it is you are doing. Candles also have the dual purpose in that some of them also are able to amplify and focus the manifestation work that you are already doing. In this way not only is your mind more focused and efficient, but the work you do is that much more effective because of the crystals themselves. Working with crystals is an art of its own, one in which the various types of crystals and the exact principles used with each one fills several large volumes. However again for our uses we will simply use them as focusing and amplifying devices.

For these uses the safest, easiest and most affordable crystal to obtain is the common clear quartz crystal. Do not worry about the size, shape or clarity for this exercise. If you are lucky enough to live in an area where quartz is naturally abundant you can simply use one of the rocks that you find lying about. If you have a particularly cherished stone feel free to use that as well. The simple steps below are easy enough to remember but can prove to be very effective, even for people who have never before used crystals for manifestation:

1. Clean your crystal by either dipping it into a salt water solution (hand-made or sea water) or set your crystal out in the light of the full moon.
2. Visualize the object of your desires in as much detail as you can manage.
3. Imagine that the object that you are visualizing is passing through the crystal and the crystal is acting as a lens to make the picture larger, brighter and in sharper focus.
4. Repeat an affirmation while holding the crystal as many times as you desire.

Obviously there are many more potential steps a person can take with crystals. As I stated earlier they are a body of work unto themselves. You can make working with them as complicated or simple as you please, and in this book we are erring on the side of simplicity. Remember that the more rules you put onto yourself or allow others to put onto you the higher the chance that you will forget them. It is much more important for the manifestation beginner to focus on what really matters, in this case their visualizations, affirmations and goals, than arcane principles. I can assure you that you will not anger any beings or manifest "wrong" if you keep it simple and stick to the four steps above. If you feel guided to add or remove any steps please feel free to do so. The method that works best is the method that works for you.

Beyond the physical items such as candles and pads of paper there are exercises that you can perform that will help you keep a focus on your life and your manifestations. Yoga is an increasingly popular method of sharpening the body and mind and I do recommend the practice if you feel it is right for you. Other people, me included, benefit more from regular Tai Chi sessions. Tai Chi has the added benefit of being freely available in public parks worldwide. If there is a public park of sufficient size in your town or city there is a very good chance that Tai Chi groups meet on a regular basis during warm weather months. The reason Yoga and Tai Chi help you improve your focus is that in addition to being wonderful exercises for the body, they are also meditative in nature. Meditating in any form helps bring our mind into sharp focus by being constantly exercised and trained. While it is perfectly acceptable and quite beneficial to simply meditate, doing so in a Yoga or Tai Chi setting has the added benefit of physical exercise. Physical exercise is well known to promote increased concentration and memory retention when performed regularly and the meditation benefit will be cumulative when they are performed together.

There will be times when you lose your focus regardless of how well trained your mind is, how thorough your notes are and how centered you may be. Do not panic when this happens, it is perfectly natural. That is simply your subconscious telling you that you should focus on something else at this time. Sometimes we are meant to think about the distracting thoughts that enter our mind. Take a moment to sort through them, and if any need to be taken care of straight away go ahead and take care of them. The rest will quiet down with contemplation and acknowledgement, and you will be able to go back to your manifestation work with a clear head and focused mind. Losing focus is not the end of the world; it is simply an opportunity to re-evaluate your priorities at that particular moment.

The difference between a manifestation done with a focused mind and a manifestation done with an unfocused mind is similar to the difference between music played by a master, and one played by a first year student. The manifestation is still being done, but with far more efficiency and much more desirable results. This is why I encourage you to establish what it is that is distracting your focus and eliminating it from your mind as soon as possible.

If you just try to power through the visualization or affirmation while thinking about how the washing needs to be done, the kids need to be fed and the dog needs to be walked you will essentially be wasting your time. Of course you will never be able to set yourself back by any measure and no one is keeping track but you, but you owe it to yourself to be fully focused whenever you set out to manifest this abundance that is coming your way.

A simple way to focus yourself when you are finding your mind cluttered with other tasks that can be safely left until later is to say this quick blessing to yourself: "My life is one of abundance; an abundance of joy, love, blessings and free of any worry. I deserve to grow this abundance in order to grow and make the world a better place."

This simple blessing above reminds us that it is okay to be abundant, that we are already abundant and that we want nothing but goodness for everyone with our increased abundance. The tasks that can wait until later are safely left behind, because you are focused on a much bigger project at that particular moment. You are a very important person and must allow yourself the time it takes to do your job and to do it properly.

Starting today and continuing on for as long as it takes for you to feel comfortable, I would like you to repeat that blessing above. Feel free to make a little note, tick mark or number in your journal at the back of this book every day that you repeat it. Think of how you feel the very first time you say it. Compare that to how you feel the tenth day of saying it. See how long it takes for you to actually believe it. It will be at that point that you will really be able to keep focus, no matter what others tell you or what you have previously told yourself.

This chapter is called "Keeping Focus" but it very well could have been called "Giving Yourself Permission" because that really is what keeping your focus is. It is your mind giving you permission to be as abundant as you want to be. There will always be an excuse or something better that you could be doing, but by giving yourself permission you are reminding yourself that you are just as important to look after as everyone else around you. Instead of thinking about all of the things that you could be doing instead or about how guilty you feel for taking time for yourself, think about all of the good things you will be able to do with the abundance that you are working so hard to obtain. Ultimately you and everyone else around you will be much better off because you took the time out of your busy schedule to focus on you.

Since you are now in the habit of keeping notes it is also a good idea to take a moment now and again to brainstorm new ideas that you have. Every single device or service that you use every day started out life as a single idea in someone's head. They were no different than you, they just pushed ahead with that idea despite everyone telling them how quickly and painfully it would fail. Once you start coming up with these great ideas you can start focusing on them, visualizing them and affirming that these ideas are realities and are making people happy and you lots of well-deserved income. Nearly every single part of your day can be used to manifest abundance in some manner or another. We are constantly surrounded by the wonder of creation, and so too can we also create. When you have trained your mind to the point when you can keep focus on what it is that you want regardless of external distractions you can easily take five minutes to do a quick visualization wherever you happen to be. Say you are stuck in a dull meeting that has absolutely nothing whatsoever to do with your job responsibilities (don't laugh, it does happen) well then that is just a perfect time to either silently repeat affirmations or to visualize the object of your desires. Not only will this ground you and center you but it will at the very least make the time you are spending in this meeting worthwhile.

When you start to practice manifesting during times when you otherwise would be idle you start to reclaim so-called "wasted time." If you were so inclined to keep track of how much time you are able to snatch away for manifestation you would be quite surprised how much time you have managed to get back.

As I stated earlier a lot of this work is residual, so you may not notice effects right away and you may not notice the effects diminish right when you stop practicing. One of the most important aspects of manifestation then must be consistency. I would not go so far as to say that stopping right when things start working for you would be foolish, but it would be at least wasteful of your effort. Once you decide to start back up again you will once again have to wait out the lag time until it starts working again. It would be far better to simply continue your practice without stopping then to constantly restart. This will save not only time but also keep your mind used to using all of the manifestation tools at your disposal. Keeping up your practice is the ultimate method of keeping your focus.

Chapter Six

Staying Positive

Positivity is the language of heaven. When we speak and think in positive ways we are having a direct conversation with our creator. The Angels of Abundance are delighted when we choose to look at all situations as potentially positive. After all, everything is happening according to a divine plan so the end result is of course positivity.

We recognize this instinctually. How many times has someone said to you, "We'll be laughing about this later." That is an inherent acknowledgment that all things are destined to work out for the best in the end. God and the angels really are looking out for our highest good at all times and a positive outlook is nothing more than recognition of this fact.

When we remain positive about our manifestations we are able to realize much stronger and more significant gains. The positivity and enthusiasm that we possess translates directly into more effective manifestation sessions. Conversely if we lose that positivity and start doubting the effectiveness of our practice or start turning negative towards the work that we are trying to do we can lose progress or even stop it completely.

The reason behind this shifting based on our positivity or negativity has to do with the energy that our thoughts and words contain. In one of my previous works, "Angel Words", it was demonstrated that positive words have a much higher amount of energy than negative words. This means that your positive thoughts and emotions lend energy to your manifestation work, and indeed every aspect of your life, and lead to much higher levels of effectiveness.

Conversely negative thoughts and emotions carry very little energy. This means that while negativity is not outright harmful or dangerous it is quite useless.

On a practical level positivity can lead to much more fulfilling relationships with other people. Very people, yourself likely included, want to spend very much time around a person who is negative most of the time. It can be a real drag to be around and can negatively affect the mood of everyone around them. On a natural and instinctive level people naturally shy away from someone that they feel is negative. When we strive to stay positive not only do we tend to have more energy but we are much more enjoyable to be around.

Obviously staying positive just for the sake of keeping people around is not the primary goal and should not be the only reason for staying positive. The fact of the matter is that every single possible area of your life can be improved by a positive mindset. Your health, happiness and even prosperity can be dramatically improved by shifting your focus around to notice all of the positive events and occurrences in your life rather than focusing solely on the negative.

It can be difficult to stay positive in the face of adversity, but it is not impossible. The health, happiness and wealth benefits aside staying positive is just more effective for every area of your life. If you go into a venture with an optimistic feeling and attitude you are much more likely to succeed. Whoever heard of anyone going into a venture knowing that it is going to fail and still giving it one-hundred percent? When we revert to negativity we are effectively sabotaging ourselves.

Failing to acknowledge danger or potentially negative situations does no one any good. Staying positive does not mean living in your own under-water bubble city, oblivious to the world around you. Yes, it is a good idea to avoid doom and gloom news shows or newspapers, but staying completely uninformed of the world is not an abundance gaining habit. In order to keep up with what is new and what potential knowledge you need to gain to stay competitive in your chosen field. If a situation is potentially dangerous or hostile failing to acknowledge that fact will not help improve matters. You must be realistic in order to stay happy, healthy and wealthy. Realistic, however, does not have to turn into negativity.

How can we stay positive when we are potentially surrounded by a negative world? Easy, and the first step is not to think of the world as negative. The world certainly has problems but they are not insurmountable. Most of the world's problems are manmade and can be man-solved. By acknowledging that we can fix any problem given enough thoughtful care it becomes much easier to avoid the trap of despair. The second step is to keep track of all of the beauty, goodness and blessings that you notice around you. Lord knows that enough of the negative actions of this world are chronicled, so why not the positive?

We call this documenting of goodness a "gratitude journal." I know, you may have visions of a love-in back in the sixties but this really is a valuable tool in keeping positive. You do not have to make any larger of a spectacle about it than you want to. A gratitude journal can be as complicated as a leather bound tome that you fastidiously keep notes in, to an application on your smart phone. Yes, they have an app for that. At first you may not notice or remember every single bit of goodness that comes your way, but that is perfectly fine. The more you use a gratitude journal the more you will notice.

At a certain point you may start to question whether all of this goodness has always been there, or is more coming to you because of your work and the fact that you are, at last, acknowledging its presence? Like most of life, the answer is all of the above. Yes there has always been wonderful and beautiful things in this world but they have a tendency to be overshadowed by the negative and dangerous things, but just as like-attracts-like, the more you align yourselves with good the more good will come to you.

If this all sounds too good to be true you should ask yourself why you believe that to be the case. Yes, we do live in a cynical world and there are people that would try to take advantage of your trusting nature, but that is not the way of God and the universe. Our divine creator wants us to be abundant and happy just as we want our children to be abundant and happy. The only thing limiting us is our belief that we are in this world by ourselves.

Losing motivation can be a serious impediment to your manifestation work. We can lose motivation when we do not feel that we are making progress quickly enough. If your friends and family are not being supportive of you that can also make it easier to lose motivation. Staying positive will help you retain that motivation. If you feel that your progress is not going as quickly, consult your gratitude journal. You will quickly start to notice that the number of positive things in your life has drastically improved.

If you feel that your friends and family are not being supportive enough then you should speak with them about this. Most likely they were not even aware that you felt this way and will take steps to resolve the situation with you. You do not want to simply let it sit with them and hope that the situation improves itself. This is a breakdown in communication and it serves no one. If you keep the communication channels open with your loved ones you can stop these issues before they become larger problems or real rifts in your relationship.

It can be a very uplifting experience to share your personal ambitions with those closest to you. You should never feel guilty or ashamed of what you want to manifest. You, out of everyone that you know, are in the best place to know what it is that you need in your life. Other people may have valuable suggestions but ultimately only you can make a decision that something is for your highest good.

If you feel that you have lost motivation to continue in your manifestation work a great tool to use is something called a "vision board." What this is is a poster that you make that contains pictures and positive words that are you short or long term goals. You can have pictures of a beautiful home, symbols of wealth such as fancy cars or jewelry, and positive affirmations about your abundance.

When you look at your vision board you are reminded what it is that you are hoping to achieve and hopefully will see how your continued perseverance is worth the effort. If you do not see something that really motivates you on the board, then tear down the unexciting pictures and put up something that will really get you fired up.

The act of being positive has a cumulative effect in your life. The more positive, motivated and enthusiastic you are about your life in general and your manifestations specifically the more success and happiness you will be able to achieve. While it is certainly possible for negative people to achieve success it would have been that much easier for them had they kept a positive attitude.

In real world, applications a person's attitude can open and close a great deal of doors. When trying to a new job, a higher position, or transferring departments in a traditional employer a great deal of weight is placed on a person's general attitude towards work and life in general. Even when a person is self-employed they will have a great deal more success dealing with customers and suppliers when they keep a positive attitude.

Some people may feel that I am trying to tell them that they can never have a bad day or have to pretend to be positive all the time. This is most certainly not the case. I understand all too well that life sometimes can interfere with our intentions. When we are confronted with bad news or a sudden turn of fate it can be easy to slip into a more negative state of mind. All I ask is that you be consciously aware of those times and try to limit their scope.

When we are consciously aware of ourselves at every moment we can obtain a realistic view of our lives. In that case we can see for ourselves where our energy is being spent. If you are fully aware of the times when you are positive and when you are negative then you can get a better idea of the cause and effect that each of these attitudes is having in our lives. At that point we are more qualified to make an informed decision about what reaction we choose to have to any given situation.

Yes, we can choose how we react to situations. It may seem that we are merely reacting to the situation in the most appropriate manner at the time, but that moment is our choice just as any others are. If you think back on a particularly stressful situation you were involved in try imagining how someone you really respect would have reacted. Would they have reacted in a more positive or more negative situation, or do you imagine they would have reacted in a similar manner to yourself?

The point of that exercise is to see that there is no "most appropriate" reaction to any given stimuli. The only gauge of appropriateness is how your reaction made you feel. If you feel guilty or sick over your reaction then that was not the right one for you to choose. On the other hand if you feel uplifted and good about how you reacted then that was the correct decision.

We can train ourselves to react in a way in which we consciously choose. We do this by taking very small steps towards being constantly aware that we are in fact making a choice. The next time you are faced with a stressful or surprising situation try this instead: breath before acting. Take five to ten seconds to calm and center yourself before you have any sort of outward reaction. Once you have calmed and centered yourself by breathing see if you still feel inclined to behave in the same manner as you initially would have.

If that seems overly simplified to you, ask yourself why you believe that to be the case? We train ourselves by repeatedly performing tasks. In this case the only thing that we are trying to train ourselves is to think before acting. Nothing could be simpler. Once we have gotten skilled in this art then we are free to make any decision that we would like, but we start to become aware of those choices.

Most people find that when they start becoming aware of not only the consequences of a choice but the fact that they have a choice at all they will choose correctly more often. Not coincidentally what is the correct choice for most people is to react to each situation in a more positive manner. Not only is it usually the much more successful choice but it also feels better. While the idea of really getting angry with someone and letting them have it can be fun or satisfying in some ways, the real truth of the matter is that it rarely feels good if we ever do actually indulge in that impulse.

The bridge between positive thoughts and positive actions is very small. Most people find that what they primarily choose with one will usually translate to the other. For example it is a very rare situation that someone who consistently thinks positively will regularly choose to act negatively. That would be a thought-action mismatch that can certainly last for a time but would eventually be overridden. Our thoughts become our actions and, just as often, our actions can become our thoughts.

Everyone has a certain default set of actions that they typically engage in. These patterns come about through a combination of your past experiences, upbringing, moral values and general personality. Actions that are in line with your personality generally happen much faster and with less effort. They are more akin to habits than conscious choices. Conversely actions that go against your personality can cause a thought-action mismatch.

Going through a thought-action mismatch is not necessary a bad thing. In some circumstances we have allowed ourselves to be pre-programmed with a set of actions that does not serve either ourselves or the world. When we recognize that this is case we must realign ourselves to a new set of default actions.

The desire to want to align ourselves in more positive ways is a common one. For example some people gradually come to the conclusion that they are more of an angry person than they would rather be. Realizing that becoming a calmer, happier person not only improves their interpersonal relationships but also can improve their health and longevity; these people desire to change their personality. It does not have to just be harmful personalities such as anger that people desire to change. If you have ever felt that you are too passive, accommodating, or are possessing any other personality trait that you feel is no longer serving you, you can change that.

Realigning personality traits is a surprisingly easy task. With a small amount of discipline even the most ingrained impulses can be mastered and corrected. There have been countless stories published of very negative people having epiphanies and turning their lives around completely. These people are not special in a way that the rest of us are not, they simply had a desire to turn their life around and attract more positive people and circumstances.

The first step to any transformation is awareness. If or when you recognize something about yourself that you would like to change you have already completed the most important, and in some ways difficult, steps toward completing that goal. What follows is gradually becoming more aware of those times when you display the behavior that you feel no longer serves you.

When you notice your actions you can choose to interrupt your thought-action flow and introduce a new element into it. Rather than act in the more negative manner that would otherwise have been the default action we can instead experiment with the more positive option. It is highly probable that the result of this little experiment will help remind you to stay positive even when things start to feel as if they are sliding towards the negative.

 The most important thing to remember is that you are not alone. Your divine creator, the Angels, your friends, and your family are all supporting you every step of the way. There is no situation that cannot be improved by looking at it with a positive outlook. Your positivity and   forward thinking attitude are investments that you are making in yourself.

Chapter Seven

The Contract

At the start of this book I mentioned that this was a book about contracts. These contracts are between you and your divine creator. The angels play a very important role in this contract.

The interesting thing about this contract is that it is so incredibly one sided. You are contracting to receive exactly what you ask to receive. You are not expected to give anything back, except for perhaps a touch of appreciation and acknowledgment of where your blessings are coming from.

The Angels of Abundance relay your wishes, amendments and desires on to the universal power where they are being fulfilled. You have learned throughout this book the importance of making sure that the message that is being passed on is exactly what you'd like it to be. At no point was I trying to scare you by illustrating the importance of specificity.

Instead I was merely passing on a truth that you need to be aware of in order to fully make and understand your choices.

Awareness is the key to so many areas of our lives. Without it we may as well be drones. All of your choices must be made with full knowledge of why you are making them. Even if the reason for your choice is not the best, having one and being aware of it is what matters.

One of the trickiest areas of this subject is how your choices affect other people. It is true that sometimes our choices can bring negative consequences on people we care about. The angels teach us, however, that if we are truly aware of the extent of our choices that will never happen. It is part of our lesson here on Earth to learn how to anticipate the consequences of our choices and actions until completion.

Consequences do not have a limitless chain of events following them. Like a stone thrown in a large lake, the energy of your actions does eventually return back to neutral. This is great news for us as the human mind can have trouble with the concept of infinity from time to time. This also means that given enough thoughtful intention you can reasonably foresee how your choices will impact others.

It is my belief that it is a very rare person who deliberately sets out to harm others. For the most part people are good hearted and kind. The majority of hurt and pain that are caused by our fellow humans is therefore unintentional. When we raise our awareness we in turn act as a beacon to show others how to raise their awareness as well.

The Angels of Abundance love it when we show others how to become more aware of their choices. They know that they have to pass on whichever messages we give to them, whether we know we are giving them one or not. When we are more aware they are able to pass on loving messages that will help us immensely. Given the choice everyone prefers to pass on positive news and requests than negative ones.

The nature of these contracts that we make with our divine creator can change over time. If we come to an epiphany and decide that the current track of our life is unacceptable to us or needs to be improved in some way we are free to change that. Using the tools outlined in this book it is entirely possible to effortlessly change every area of your life for the better.

The nature of time as it exists on our planet is purely a human construct. You may believe that because you have lived your life in a set pattern for so long that it may take you a proportional amount of time to change your life. That is simply not true. Your life is assisted by divine beings that are not limited to space and time in any way. They will help you move your life to a positive and fulfilling direction now. However, like all contracts, you must give something in return.

What could you as a human with a physical body possibly give to a spiritual being that is without limits? After all they can have anything that they desire at any time, if they even desired anything at all. The nature of value only exists with humans because of the finite nature of our physical plane. The spiritual plane has no such limitations so the nature of giving something in return may sound ludicrous. There is, fortunately for us, one very important thing that we can offer in return for this divine assistance.

That valuable piece of property that we can offer is called permission. God, the angels, and all of the divine beings cannot act on your behalf without you asking for help. Your right to self-rule and free-will is without limit for all eternity. Even if these otherwise limitless creations desired to subvert your free-will, and they of course never desire to do that, they would be incapable of doing so.

We were put on this planet for a very important reason. Every person's reason is different but all of them involve being able to make choices. We are faced with one thousand temptations to ignore our divine purpose every single day and what makes us great and unique gifts to the world is that we ignore those temptations. We can turn off the television, put down the game controller, and say no to that night out at the club.

You do not, of course, need to shut yourself off from life. The monastic life may be fulfilling for some, but it is not what we were put here on this Earth to accomplish. You do need, though, to be able to focus enough on working on your own projects and keeping out any potential negativity while you recreate your life in positive new ways.

You will know instantly whether or not you are in a positive contract. When you find yourself in a positive contract you must do your very best to ignore those around you who tell you that all good times must come to an end. The Buddhist mantra of "This too shall pass" may be true, but when we are speaking of divine contracts when one ends another immediately begins. The good times of positivity, abundance and love need never come to any end.

The goal of all of these contracts is to help you fine tune your life so that external distractions do not keep you from focusing on your life path. The angels do not want mundane details such as worry and lack to interfere with the lessons you are here to learn. They will absolutely help you with any area of your life where you feel you can use the assistance. You simply have to swallow your pride and ask for help.

From time to time it can feel that even though we are asking over and over again for help, and that our need is so great that we cannot understand why no help is forthcoming. This is simply a misunderstanding due to a difference in perspective on the situation. We are by necessity active participants in our lives. We see things from the first person perspective and it can be very difficult to step out into the third person perspective. God and the Angels are not limited in this regard at all. They can see every single aspect of our lives with much greater clarity and wisdom than we can imagine. If you are genuinely asking for and are open to help you are receiving it. You may not be able to fully see or appreciate the level of help you are receiving at the time but everything is being put into place for your greatest good.

I completely understand that this can be a tough message to accept at times. It can be easy to confuse what we believe to be the best for ourselves and what is truly best. This is where faith comes in. We have to be able to trust that God and the angels are looking out for us at every step of the way. Do not fret if this is difficult for you. After all, if faith was easy then it would have no value. It is by definition something that you should come by after much thought and contemplation.

Once you are through with a contract you may end it at any time. If your priorities have realigned for any reason you may simply switch to a different manifestation. You do not need to wait for each contract to finish successfully before moving on to another one. You can do this in several ways.

The first way to remove an old contract is to simply ask your angels, any will do although it is a particular specialty of Archangel Michael, to cut your cords to your old contract. A cord is essentially a spiritual tie to another object, desire, being, or thought. You develop these cords whenever you encounter any of these objects, people or thoughts. They are a method of passing energy between you and everything else in the universe. When these cords build up too densely to the point where they are literally draining your energy, or you simply no longer need the object to be in your life you can ask for them to be cut. The severing of these cords can often uplift you if you have excessive numbers of them but they never remove any positive influences from your life. You do not need to be afraid that removing your cords to your partner will negatively impact your relationship.

When you cut your cords to an old contract you are saying to the universe that you no longer wish to spend energy on that task and that you would instead like that energy redirected to the next contract. There is absolutely no penalty for canceling a contract early.

The second method for canceling an old contract that is no longer serving you is a bit more esoteric. This method is perfect for those amongst us that work better with physical objects and symbols rather than intangible thoughts. This method requires you to write down exactly what it is that you were trying to manifest or attract into your life. You may be as detailed or general as you wish. This has much more to do with your own comfort and peace of mind than it being a secret ritual that must be done in the proper order and way.

Once you have written down what you were previously trying to attract, you then bury that piece of paper under Earth of any sort. Provided that is a regular wood-based sheet of paper it will biodegrade in a matter of days. That will completely remove any residual remnant of that old contract from your life forever.

You may restart a contract if, for any reason, you change your mind. Even a contract that has been cancelled for some time may be reopened and the manifestation process continued. If you remember precisely what you were previously trying to attract, you may simply ask the angels to help you reach your goal. Otherwise you can repeat your earlier manifestation using whichever technique you used before. This should be much easier this time as you have already been through the process previously.

The word contract can sound scary to some. In this instance you have nothing to fear. You will not owe anyone anything throughout this contract. At no point will you be subject to any penalties for lack of action on your behalf. You are free to enter and leave this contract as you will. This is a contract of unconditional love that will help you achieve all of your heart's desires.

The Angels of Abundance want you to know that they absolutely want you to ask them for their help. They have infinite patience and will wait for you to request their help. You never have to worry that you are bothering them. They have no limitations on how many places they can be at once. If you are asking for their help it does not mean that they would be unable to help someone else with a more dire need. They can, and are, helping everyone with equal tenacity.

Chapter Eight

Manifestation Stories

I receive letters on a regular basis from people who have tried the techniques outlined in this book to their own great success. Many times the person in question only resorts to even trying a certain technique due to a perceived emergency or special circumstance. In a virtual act of desperation they decided to take a risk and see if there was any truth to these tools.

The results, as you may well be able to imagine, were well worth the effort and more. When we let go of our ego and decide that we have had enough and that it is okay if we ask for help there is literally no limit to how much we can achieve. The only limited person in the world, and I mean this in every way and taking into account all supposed handicaps, is the one who does not ask for help when it is needed.

One nice gentleman, Thomas from California, wrote me not long ago. He explained that he was temporarily out of work due to his company being bought out by a larger competitor. The large company decided not to keep any of the staff on after the acquisition so suddenly there were several people in his area all looking for the same job.

Thomas knew without a doubt that he was going to find a new job, but in the meantime he had bills to pay so that his family would not unduly suffer during this career transition. He went on to say that he did some simple math and quickly deduced that he did not have enough in his checking account to satisfy all of the outstanding debts. This was not a very comforting feeling for Thomas.

That very day Thomas starting using affirmations. He would repeat to himself, "I am divinely cared for in all ways. I always have enough to pay my bills." Thomas apparently believes as I do, that a simple affirmation can be very effective. He wrote out checks to his utility companies, mortgage lender, credit card and other companies with outstanding debts. He repeated his affirmation as he wrote out each check and again when he went to mail them.

Two weeks later the checks had not cleared his account. He was not receiving any harassing phone calls yet so he was not quite sure what to make of the situation. Thomas wrote that he decided that the best thing to do was to call these companies himself before they decided that his payments were not sent. Each company reported back that they had received the payments and posted them to his account. He was completely current and nothing further needed to be done at that point.

He continued to check in with his bank but the checks had never been received by them. The companies assured him that they had deposited the check, crediting his account but the money was never withdrawn from his bank account. In the end it was quite true what he said to himself; he had plenty to pay his bills.

Thomas' story, as remarkable as it was, is hardly unique amongst those who regularly practice some form of manifestation. Regardless of what area of your life you are trying to improve you will realize incredibly strong gains every single time when you use these tools.

These tools work because they are divine gifts. They are not subject to human and physical limitations. Time and distance mean nothing to the angels; they are always available and willing to help you. You are certainly not limited to the tools outlined in this book; the ones here are simply what most people find accessible and helpful for their lives. The angels are happy to pass on any loving message and call to help regardless of how it is asked.

One day a couple of years ago I received a letter from Margaret from Virginia. She told me how she desired to return to college after a two year break. Margaret wrote that she had intended to work and raise enough money to finish college during these two years. However her finances never really caught up to her expenses to the point where she could save enough money.

Margaret decided to that in order to finish her goal she would have to try something different. She decided to create a vision board. Her vision board consisted of pictures of various people graduating from college, new cars, and houses with "Sold" signs. These pictures helped clearly define and focus her goals to manageable levels. She had something to keep her mind focused on exactly what she wanted so that God and the angels could bring her exactly what she wanted.

Margaret reported that within three weeks of creating this vision board she had been promoted at work to a management position in a new town. Part of the perks of her relocating to the town was a company car, an easy mortgage in a new neighborhood the company had made arrangements with to house employees, and tuition to a night school management degree program at the local college.

God and the angels are not limited in any way, even still they have a much easier time giving us what we need and desire when we are clear what we want. When we can clearly define and speak what we want we become that much closer to achieving our goals.

The tools that we are given to manifest with can be very powerful and can be put to use in new and interesting ways. There is nothing to say that you must use these tools in prescribed ways. A letter that I received several years ago by Amanda from New York illustrated this point fairly well.

Amanda was home one night finishing up some work when the power suddenly went out. She lived in a rural area so was fortunately well prepared for such a circumstance. She lit a few emergency candles and was able to ensure that everything was well.

Amanda writes that approximately one hour later the cause for the power outage made itself known: a very large, and noisy, lightning storm. She was understandably scared. Amanda decided then and there that she no longer wished to be scared. She took her emergency candles, and imaged calm waters, clear skies and electricity on at her house. Using techniques very similar to those outlined in this book she turned her ordinary emergency candle into a powerful tool for manifestation.

Shortly after finishing this small manifestation ritual the storm moved off. The sky cleared, and she was able to see the stars and moon. Not long after the power company was able to restore electricity to all the effected homes and all was well.

Amanda's story shows us how with very little preparation and the bare minimum of tools it is possible to manifest our desires. We do not need to stand on ritual unless it helps us in some way. If the ritual has meaning to you then it is important, however if you feel that any part of the ritual is tedious or meaningless then it has no use and can be discarded. If all you have is an emergency candle, then what better candle to use in an emergency.

I have heard so many times from so many people that they are afraid that their problem would be too trivial to bother the angels with. There has never been a scenario that was true. Every situation that is distracting you from your mission is worthy of asking God and the angels for help with. You never need to worry that you are bothering the angels. They want to help you and are only waiting for you to ask.

Whenever I find myself in a bit of trouble or am worried about some event, the first thing I always try to do is to ask for help. This has not always been an easy thing for me to do. In the past I have been one of those guys who was too proud to ask for help, even when I really needed it. Getting over that hurdle is a common challenge for most men in all societies. Unfortunately there really is no easy solution to magically make you more willing to ask for help. It is your attitude towards help that must be changed. The way in which you came to your present belief or preference about asking for help is as unique and individual as the man himself.

Every single person can get to the place where they no longer find asking for help uncomfortable. Sure, there may be times when you would rather not do it because you believe that you can do it yourself just as easy. That is not the same as being completely shut down to the idea. The only effective method known to become comfortable with this very important job is to keep asking for help. Every single time if possible. The more you ask, the more comfortable with asking you will become. I can attest that in my case it took several years of constantly reminding myself to ask before I became comfortable with it.

The reward is, of course, worth the effort. When we ask God and the angels, including the Angels of Abundance, for help we receive it every single time. As stated previously the help may not be in an instantly recognizable form but in the end you will receive exactly the level of help that you need. If you choose not to ask for help then the level of assistance that God and the angels are able to give you is drastically limited. All of us were given free will and that includes the right to try to make it in this world without any divine intervention whatsoever.

The majority of people would find that a life without any help from above would not be the type of life that they would strongly desire for themselves. It cannot be stated enough times how important and effective simply asking for help is.

One letter we received from a man named Dennis from London illustrated the above points remarkably well. Dennis was a taxi driver and always fancied himself a man's man who could do anything himself. Most of the time he was quite correct in this assumption, and so he continued on into old age. However, as some people do, Dennis started getting to the stage where doing everything by himself was increasingly difficult. Dennis writes that despite the fact that he clearly was in need of assistance with several areas of his life, he found himself completely incapable of asking for help. Even when help was offered he still refused because that would be an admission of weakness from his point of view.

Fortunately for Dennis he was gifted with a wonderful dream, in which all of his family was together and happy. In this dream he was able to help out his family to the best of his ability, and his family helped him out in return. He was able to see the many ways in which his family was grateful to him for all of his years of hard work and dedication, and he in turn was learning how proud he was of his family for being so close and willing to help.

From that day forward Dennis was no longer afraid of asking for help. He would perform tasks such as he was able to but if something was too difficult for him to do he would ask for help. Eventually this led to him to going so far as to ask for divine intervention on behalf of himself and various family members. Dennis goes on to write that without that dream, of which he credits the angels for giving him, he would most likely not have connected to such a large degree with his family and God. He believes that there would have been a good chance that had he continued on his old path he may not even be alive any longer.

In some ways Dennis' story is an extreme one, but in other ways it is something that most of us will face sooner or later. Everyone will come to a point where we absolutely have no other choice but to ask for help and we must be comfortable enough to do that without hesitation. Dennis was able to break through that barrier and was rewarded with a fulfilling, comfortable and safe elderly life. Imagine what sort of surprises are in store for you when you ask for help as well.

When asking for help from above you may, from time to time, be required to act on the help that is offered to you. If you ask for a new job and are suddenly called into an interview, you cannot skip the interview and be expected to be given the job. In that case you will have to do some legwork of your own. In many cases the help you are given is the equivalent of God opening a door; you have to walk through.

Chapter Nine

Meditations for Abundance

Meditations are very important tools for manifesting abundance. When you use meditations you can quickly align yourself to the positive energies of abundance. What you focus on during your meditation can directly effect on the end result of your manifestations. It is therefore very important that you only focus on very positive and loving images and thoughts.

Included in this chapter are several sample meditations that you can use to help start you on the way towards manifesting abundance. Feel free to modify any of these meditations to suit your needs. If there is a particular bit of imagery that you would prefer to have included as well, you can either replace parts of the meditation or even add it into the middle. The only thing that is asked of you is for you to think before you add anything. Is this particular bit of imagery as positive as it can be? Are you absolutely certain that you want to manifest this? If the answer to both of these questions is yes, you may add your addition in without fear.

The first of these meditations calls upon the Angels of Abundance to help you start to manifest your desires. You start and end this meditation through breath.

Breathe slowly but deeply, in through the mouth and out through the nose. Repeat this breath seven times. Imagine that with each breath you are expelling all fear and doubt from your body, while in taking pure hope and positivity.

Continue breathing slowly as you call into being a picture in your mind of what it is you would like to manifest. Try to call this picture into being with as much detail as possible. See every aspect of this object as if it was physical. Hold this picture in your mind, ignoring all external distractions. The only thing that is real at this moment is your picture and your breath.

While still holding this picture in your mind, mentally or verbally say the following few phrases:

"Angels of Abundance please come to me now. I ask for your help to continue on my life path without physical distraction and discomfort. I realize that my path is a powerful one and would like to focus completely upon it without worry.

I trust that God and the angels will help me with these goals as they help everyone who asks. I have no doubt or fear in my heart. Please ensure that my desires and needs are met in all ways and always.

Thank you God and Angels of Abundance for providing such loving bounty now. I reaffirm my desire to continue the path that God and myself have chosen to better the planet in the most effective way.

Amen."

Now simply be at peace and focus on your breath. Every breath is a gift from God and reminds us that we are abundantly provided for in so many different ways. To God all abundance is the same. God and the angels will provide equally for all.

Stay at peace and breathe for as long as you desire. You may end this meditation at any time. Some people like to repeat this meditation over again. Whichever you choose, come in peace and go in peace. This is not the place for fear or doubt. It is an absolute truth that God and the Angels will do what is best for you now that you have asked.

It is important to note that you can think of more than one object to manifest during your meditations. The only limitations here are from your own ego. The power of the divine is limitless and so you should not limit yourself. If you wish to manifest a house, a car, and a great new job then by all means try to manifest all three of those at the same time. You do not need to wait for one manifestation to come into physical being before starting on the next.

If you are having troubles focusing on multiple objects at once then simply perform this meditation one after another until you have started on all three. You simply need to be able to stay positive, have faith, remember to ask and all of your physical wants and needs will be taken care of.

If there is something very specific that you would like, such as a particular house that you have had your eye on, then specificity can be very helpful. When you picture the house in your mind try visualizing the outside walls. Imagine what it would feel like to actually touch that house. What does the house smell like? Has it got a lawn? Picture yourself mowing the lawn and imagine the feeling that you would have when you were doing so.

All of those added touches make the picture more real and believable to your mind. The more real the manifestation is the easier it is to bring it into physical being. This happens because you are more likely to believe that the object is real if you can make it feel real. Real objects to us are things that we can see, touch, smell, taste and hear. If this object in your mind can include all of these five senses there is nothing that is separating it from what is physically real.

You can see then that when you meditate you will nearly always utilize the techniques learned in earlier chapters. This whole body approach towards manifestation has been proven several times over again to be the most effective method currently known. Eventually more effective methods will be discovered, and results can and do vary wildly depending on the individual. With enough practice you will discover which methods of manifestation you are most comfortable with.

The following meditation was kindly donated to this project by my wife, Melissa Virtue. Melissa has performed these lovely meditations for audiences around the world. She regularly guides our listeners on our weekly radio show through similar meditations. She has specifically written this meditation for you, the reader of this book. Enjoy.

"Find a comfortable, quite place you can relax. Either sit or lie down with your palms open to the sky. Close your eyes.

Take a deep inhale. Exhale releasing all air. Repeat this two more times.

In your mind's eye see a glowing emerald green light moving up from the earth into the bottom of your feet. This light feels warm and soothing. As you continue to inhale and exhale allowing the rhythm of your breath to flow, feel the emerald light moving up into your leg, hips, pelvis area, stomach, rib cage and settle into your heart space. Feel this warm light cleanse and clear your heart space. It feels as if your heart is expanding with each inhale and exhale.

Now, you see a shimmering silver ball of light floating down into the crown of your head, down into your throat area and settling into your heart space where it fuses with the green light. You can feel this beautiful silvery green light pulsing as it opens, aligns and balances your heart chakra.

As the light continues to connect you to the earth and sky, you see in your mind's eye a stone archway before you. Notice the lush growth of flowers and plants along this gateway. Take a moment to see your name etched at the top of the arch. Next to your name reads "Receives Abundance Now." This is your personal gateway to allowance. Your choice to cross this threshold sings a resounding yes to the Universe. It tells the Source you are in fact ready to receive your abundance now. You are willing to open to your bliss and abundance in all areas of your life now. You are willing to allow your highest good into your life now. Stepping through this archway, you discover a golden pathway.

Standing on this pathway is an Angel of Abundance. Take a moment to look at this angel. Do you recognize them? Ask the angel's name. They are here to guide you along your path of abundance. You begin walking the path with this angel of abundance. You may want to take note of your surroundings as you walk along the path. You may hear the tinkling of bells, the plucking of harp strings, the low heartbeat of a drum or the peaceful lapping of water. Allow your sense to open. Take in all of the blessings around you. Give thanks for them.

Ahead you begin to see a blossoming garden. As the path of abundance leads you into the heart of this vibrant garden, you see shafts of sunlight shining through the trees onto the flowers. You feel safe, protected and peaceful. You see a small crystal stone circle in the middle of the garden. Your angelic guide prompts you forward into the circle. The crystals are small enough to sit on. You may see peridot, pink quartz, amethyst, cinnabar or jade crystal seats.

Look around and choose your seat. In the center of this circle is a large selenite stone. You see the stone begin to glow and before it appears the Angels of Abundance.

Archangel Jophiel steps forward and places one hand upon your heart and one hand upon the top of your head. Listen now as she shares a message with you.
Archangel Jophiel steps behind you as Archangel Michael steps forward to place one hand on your heart and one hand on the top of your head. Listen now to Michael's message.

Archangel Michael steps behind you as Archangel Raphael steps forward placing one hand on your heart and one hand on the top of your head. Listen now to Raphael's message.

Archangel Raphael steps behind you as Archangel Metatron steps forward. He places one hand on your heart and one hand on the top of your head. Listen now to Metatron's message.

Archangel Metatron steps behind you as Archangel Raziel steps forward. He places one hand on your heart and one hand on the top of your head. Listen now to Raziel's message.

The angels begin forming a circle around you. These Angels of Abundance have attuned and aligned you to your abundance as you have asked for this. Give them thanks for their help, support and guidance.

You will receive your abundance now in all areas of your life in all ways that are for your highest good.

Gently, the light from the angels of abundance grows brighter, encasing you in warmth, security, peace, love and blessings. Know that anytime you can call upon these Angels of Abundance for help.

Breathing in this light you are ready to bring your awareness back to this time, this place, now. On your own time, bring movement back into your toes and fingers. When you are ready, gently open your eyes."

It is important to remember to be very gentle on yourself after you perform a meditation such as Melissa's above. Do not feel that you need to rush off and start a project right away. You have not wasted any time that must be made up for by working doubly hard for the next few hours. This is very important work that you deserve and owe to yourself. Take time to decompress, relax and let the messages you have received absorb.

Conclusion

Congratulations! You now have a very firm grasp on manifestation in all of its diverse forms. Every area of your life can benefit from the tools and techniques you have just learned. By completing this book in its entirety you have shown a firm commitment to not only making your life better and easier, but to improving the world as a whole.

You came to this planet to fulfill a very powerful mission. God and the angels, especially the Angels of Abundance that you have been working so closely with, are helping you every step of the way. Now that you know how to invite them in and ask them for the help you need your mission is that much closer to being fulfilled.

The Angels of Abundance are thrilled that you have taken the time to understand how they are here to help you. They do not want you to have any physical suffering due to lack. They want you to be able to complete your mission and help as many people as possible.

This book does not contain the entirety of the secrets of manifestation. There are other techniques, and if you come across any that you prefer you are certainly invited to use them. This book is essentially a 101 course on manifestation. The choice of whether or not you wish to seek out other techniques, or stay with the ones included in this book is yours and yours alone.

The most effective manifestation tool in the known universe is the one that works for you. I highly encourage you to try all of the techniques you have learned about at least once and see what you are most comfortable with. If you enjoy them all, fantastic! If, on the other hand, you felt strongly drawn to one then by all means use that one to the exclusion of all others. You are under no obligation to use any technique that you find unwieldy or uncomfortable.

In the introduction I stated that this is a book about contracts. That remains true to the end. Your end of the contract now requires you to practice in order to get results. You are equipped with the knowledge and the motivation to manifest whatever it is that you desire. It is up to you to now go on and make it happen. The Angels of Abundance are only able to help you when you ask them to. Calling upon them regularly is the ideal method of ensuring that you are never without their loving help and guidance.

Remaining open to the gifts that God and the Angels of Abundance are bringing to you is a critical piece of manifestation. You must learn to instinctively trust that the abundance coming your way is a gift from the divine. When opportunity comes your way do not pause and consider whether or not you deserve it or are worthy of it. You absolutely are. Sometimes, as in the case of job interviews or amazing deals on something you were going to purchase anyway, there is a distinct time limit involved. You must be ready to strike while the iron is hot, as the old saying goes.

If you do accidently let one of these opportunities slip by, do not despair or panic. There will be more where those came from. Once you start on the road to manifestation it can almost feel as if there is a conspiracy to make you successful and abundant. Obviously the more closely attuned you are to noticing these opportunities as they come up the better off you will be, but you should never berate yourself for missing something.

The last several pages in this book are designed to be a journal for your personal use. You can either write directly on those pages or use a separate journal if you require more space. In this journal you can write about your experiences manifesting. You can, for instance, chronicle each abundant manifestation that comes to you as you use these techniques.

Journaling helps with manifestation because it serves as a reminder. For example, if you were to chronicle forty days of manifesting and forty days of success you would instantly know why nothing happened on that forty-first day when you forgot to use your affirmations or pray.

Lastly, it would not be a Grant Virtue book if I did not include a little blurb about balance. Balance is the key to a fulfilled life. Throughout your journey you must strive to ensure that you are not giving disproportionate amounts of time or energy into any one area of your life. Abundance and success are very important, true, but they are not the most important things in life.

Make doubly sure that you do not spend all of your time working. Go for a walk on a sunny day. Watch a bit of television with someone you care for. Even go so far as to waste a little time now and again. We have all seen those people who care for nothing beyond work and seek a method of monetizing even the smallest of hobbies. It is not pretty because it is a life out of balance.

A balanced life will be of a direct benefit to your manifestations. It is a falsehood that someone must work single mindedly towards a goal to reach success. When your life is balanced in all ways it allows you to keep that positive mindset necessary to properly manifest abundance in all areas of your life. A person who works non-stop may have a financially abundant life, but at what cost to the abundance in their health and love life?

I am by no means advocating laziness. Anyone who wants to have any success in manifesting will have to work, and work very hard at times, to reach their financial goals. It is not sufficient to wish for abundance without putting any effort behind it. However the last thing that I want for anyone is for the quest for abundance taking over every aspect of their lives.

I will leave you with this: We are all made up of equal parts mind, body and spirit. In each day strive to give equal attention to each areas of your life and you will have perfect balance.

Thank you for reading,

Grant Virtue

Journal

About the Author

Grant Virtue is a fifth-generation metaphysician who has studied candle magic and music theory throughout his life. He is the Technical Coordinator for Angel University, and he plays and records meditation music. Grant currently lives with his wife and cat on the Big Island of Hawaii

Website: www.GrantVirtue.com
Twitter: @GrantVirtue

Also by Grant Virtue

Living a Blessed Life

Angel Words: Visual Evidence of How Words can be Angels in Your Life

Angel Blessings Candle Kit

Available from Hay House, Inc

www.hayhouse.com

CPSIA information can be obtained at www.ICGtesting.com
Printed in the USA
LVOW101552270112

265900LV00001B/104/P